There is a path which no fowl
knoweth, and which the vulture's
eye hath not seen.

~ Job 28: 7
The Bible: King James Version

A handsome pair of wolves
recline on the opposite bank—
nervous, alert, resting
alongside the icefall.
A green flash, a blue flash,
the stars feel very near,
and you and your fellow travelers
turn east, toward home.

~ Amy Gerstler,
Four Meditations on an Ice
Puddle, IV
in *Crown of Weeds*

FLARE PATH

ISBN 978-1481063371

Goldfinch Press, London, Ontario

The book is set in Garamond

Cover photograph by Judith Castle
Author photograph by Simon Minshall
Book Layout and Cover Design: SpicaBookDesign
Printed and bound with www.createspace.com

FLARE PATH

Poems

Judith Castle

GOLDFINCH PRESS
LONDON, ONTARIO

for my son Simon
and
in memory of my son Nathan

also
in memory of Rosemarie

Contents

Flare Path

Crazy hues, raving blare,
rhododendrons blooming
sky-loud spring, ripe buds breaking open.
Noon in the park.

It must be sea-light reflected
that pours such reckless scarlet,
violent mauve from swollen buds, throws
these dangerous colours into the play-lot
where toddlers ride shrieking
down the red tin slide, climb
the purple ladder again
and again.

I could stop walking to watch
these flushed trees hurl their radiance
across the grass, but the glare,
the ongoing explosion of petals
might leave me blind and deaf
on my pale path.

Sunday Afternoon

Heat licks the starched collar
of my Sunday dress.
This cement step is hard as a pew
and I don't care if my white ribbons lie
in the dirt where I threw them.
I'm busy digging an ant hill
with a popsicle stick I found
on the ground, the orange all melted.

Look! Here come the ants
after my earthquake. There they go,
millions in an ant parade
running down the hot sidewalk
dropping white eggs.

They can't live in a broken nest
anymore, had to leave their babies behind.
And it's all my fault they'll have to find
a new place to live, far far away
near Daddy's house, not here
where I sit watching God's ants flee
under my Sunday shoes.
Goodbye, ants! Goodbye.

Look at my hands! Dirty as sin.
I wipe them on my white dress
anyway. So there!

Doll

My china doll lies
in the shade of my palm
her smile eggshell frail
her gaze open as blue stars.

Mother tells me
I might stop playing
with dolls this summer.
I might change
into a woman in this heat,
perhaps by August, she says,
it won't hurt.

From my bedroom window I see
how sun swells the tomatoes
in my father's garden
pulls hollyhocks taller
against the wall
of the house.

I hold my doll close
like a secret I'm afraid
I'll forget if my hands grow
too big to remember.

Breath

We were in Grade Four
when you told our class
you found a baby in the garbage.
No way! we said.
Lucky it was summer! you said,
and showed us how you held
the baby's tiny nose, breathed
into her blue mouth
until she cried.

You ran with her to your house
but your mum was too high to care
for a baby so the police came
and wrapped her in a blanket
took her to a home.

After you moved away to your dad's,
the teacher shook her head, said
your story wasn't true.

But I didn't believe her
because I was with you that day
after school. You smeared
blue lipstick on your face, said
you couldn't breathe.

When you fell in the schoolyard,
I knelt beside you, breathed
into your mouth
until you wept.

Bicycle

A toy bicycle sits on the table—blue wheels,
blue spokes still
blue seat vacant—no hands hold
the handlebars.
The bicycle doesn't wait for the boy
who wants to be a bicycle rider,
who sits at the table
without a memory of his feet
turning pedals,
spokes humming in the air
spinning sky-blue wheels
down the summer-dust hill
forever under the open summer sky
on mountain bike tires wider
than the wheels
of the chair
where he sits reaching
for a bicycle
small as his hand.

Ritual

This is for the lady
who made a bonfire
in the backyard
one night last winter
when I was ten,

she was crazy,
she carried her clothes
out of the house
and burned them.

I watched her, unafraid,
pour kerosene into the flames.

Fragments of skirt lifted
in the trembling air, the ash of coats
blouses, shone in the heat
and fell like dark stars

where she stood nameless
at the edge of her world

listening.

Sail

A woman pins laundered sheets
on the line for sun to drink
wind to fill

like white sails billowing
over sweetgrass waving
in the field

tonight sun-drunk linens lie fragrant
on her child's moonlit bed,
spread for night sail.

The Promise

On the day he retired my father
heard the Voice.
He measured the backyard
foot by bare foot, then chopped
down the cypress to build
the boat.

From the window I watched him
lean into the sloping prow,
scan the sky for cloud, feel the air
for damp. Year after year

old friends carried him food,
brought towels for his brow.
When I read him their obituaries
he lost his balance and fell.

I began to dig his grave.

Still, he bent over the helm.
Hot winds sucked tears from his eyes,
burned the sea chart to dust.

I grew old listening
to his parched hope.

One evening into the fortieth year
of the drought, his good eye
caught a young gull's wing circle
through thunder, cloud.

Rain opened the sky. Rain poured
over my father's dying face.

I stayed through the flooded night
without stars,

and at dawn, when he begged me,
I hoisted sail.

Birthday

At the window I watch wind drive cloud
in from the sea carrying a bowl of rain
like a lover to bathe
the city's face.

Today is the three hundred and sixty-fifth day
I have poured out this year waiting
for my beloved
to come.

A Vermeer woman waits, hand resting
on a gold water jug. She glances
from window to road
wondering when
her lover will arrive.

Perhaps later someone will whisper
that her lover no longer thirsts for her
and has left Delft
for Amsterdam
with another.

My dying father asked me to call his lover
to wait with him
beside the white bed where he lay,
thin fingers curled
child-like, his face wet with longing
but I did not call.

Rain beats against my window all day,
blurring my view of the street where my lover
will come. I've grown old
but wait still, wearing
my father's face.

Hunger

Dad who came home from the war
passed through our rooms like a ghost
crying my name
as though I were lost.

When his night storm raged
I'd run into the yard so I wouldn't see
his hands hitting the walls
where he thought
I was hiding.

In the afternoon while he napped, I stole
change from the pocket of his big army jacket
hanging alone in the hall.

He didn't hear small fingers
lifting dimes and nickels, one by one,
didn't find me later at the corner store
stuffing O Henrys and Cherry Blossoms
into my mouth,

never found out
how hungry I was for Dad
who didn't come home.

Dad's Basement

Mum sold her house in St. Catharines because of the mess
in the basement, the pile of repairs Dad had abandoned
by dying. She wanted to hear his wrench turning
in the motor of the broken dryer, his hammer
banging nails into the loose leg of the wing chair.
It would've looked good in the den, she said,
beating the cushion with her cane.

Wherever she gazed, Mum saw Dad's chores:
the unwired crystal lamp that might have shone
in the hall, a chipped Moorcroft vase he didn't glue
back together, and there, sagging in a corner,
the red suitcase she might have carried
to the 1968 Baptist convention in Toronto.

*Why didn't your father fix the zipper? or the frame
for my painting of Niagara Falls?*

My brother and I emptied the basement
one Sunday in July, packed wrecked furniture
and thirty sacks of junk into the pickup
and sped to the dump where sunlit gulls cried
in crazy circles. We hurled the bags
onto the garbage hill. We couldn't throw them
far enough.

Mum lives in Saint John now.
She's glad we gave her treasures to people
who'd repair them. Sometimes she asks
who found a zipper for her good red suitcase
or a new wire for her beautiful crystal lamp.
She tells us that Dad was a born engineer.
She says, *Your father could fix anything
he touched.*

Separation

Dad's leaving, so I hang on
his army coat
dodging the back-swing
of his suitcase
down the long hall.

Mum wails at the cross
on the wall, *Stop him,
Jesus, Mary and Joseph*!
but he kicks the door open
with his boot, and there's me
behind him, slipping,
sliding down the front steps
with my doll, racing
across the snow barefoot
to the car.

I want him to take me
wherever he's going
now that the war
is over.

I'm a good girl, I call,
but he doesn't turn around
before he drives away.

Triolet

A child caught in a woman's game,
you climb a lilac tree and call.
Daddy watches, shouts your name,
holds out his arms, and down you fall.

You're a grown girl in a cherry tree.
Daddy's dead but kind new hands
open for you now you're free
to climb and fall in other lands.

As a mother now, how well you know
to lift your child from flowering trees
and let her daddy wait below
to catch the blossoms as they freeze.

Our Lady of the Sofa

I'll die this summer if my husband doesn't sell
enough Bibles to buy me an air conditioner,
and send the boys to church camp. I hear them
racing in the hall like the zebras that ran over
our missionary's hut in the village where God
sent her to serve.

If I hadn't married and had five boys,
I might have served God in a foreign village too,
instead of here on Harvard Ave below the tracks,
where I have to lock my china cabinet to protect
Mother's Wedgwood place-setting for four.

I don't know what I did to end up living
in a neighbourhood where women wear curlers
in their hair on Sunday, spend the day smoking cigarettes
while their children spray each other with hoses
and the beer-drinking husbands gamble
on the front steps.

When my husband drives us to church
in his old Chevy, Mother's gold brooch shines
on the St. Laurent jacket I found at St. Andrew's
bazaar. In the side mirror, I see her white shawl
fall over my shoulder like an angel's wing.

The boys scream and fight on the back seat
but I sit tall, and wave out the window
though no one stands on the sidewalk
to see me pass by.

Sister

My sister talks
to trees all winter

Wind howls

Inside her cottage
she splits kindling
for the stove

A column of ash
ascends

Maples also rise
like grey bones
climbing a hill

Behind the shed
snow sculpts
the rusted car with cold
artful hands

The garden sleeps

At twilight my sister runs
into the wood, her hair
a bright veil

I place heavy feet
where she has stepped

Wishing I knew how
to go with her.

Finding Jesus

Snow covers lawn, roofs and trees.
I press my fingers
to the frost inside my bedroom window
so I can see sparrows singing
in the bare branches of the lilac tree.
Mother says they sing hymns
but I hear their own song.
If they fall, Jesus sees them.

Mother found Jesus last summer.
She lost him when she was a girl
but now he's back. She tells me he bids
us shine and hallelujah, how snow
is the colour of forgiveness, and white
for hearts black as tar like mine.

Snow covers sin-scars with white,
the angel colour. Forgiveness is pardon,
like when I kick somebody's shin
or interrupt them when they're speaking,
I say oh, pardon me, which is often.
In the morning I say grace
before I eat my oatmeal to the last bunny
painted inside the bowl. At school
my friend Grace is in Grade One.
I hide toast in my pocket for sparrows.

After breakfast I make angels on the lawn
by lying down and swishing
my arms and legs for the wings.
I lie quiet to look at the sky. No planes fly
so I'm not killed like people in the war.

Father shovels snow on the steps
to the clothesline platform, pours
water over the snow to make ice for a slide.

After school I pull my sleigh
up the snow ramp and zoom down
fast as a bomb over the white garden,
over snow white as forgiveness for sins,
but scars are still there, like when I fall
and skin my knees playing baseball.
Jesus got killed but rose alive again.
He never plays in snow or slides
on an icy slide. He lives in a hot country.
His father isn't his real father,
his real father is God
and doesn't hammer nails
to make a platform
to the clothesline like my father.
Jesus doesn't have to walk to church
on cold Sunday mornings
or leave for war like my father.
My father should find Jesus
before he goes to war.
That's what Mother tells him,
but he says there's already enough Jesus
for one house. My father
finds beer delicious.
That's why he doesn't find Jesus.

When our milkman leaves bottles
on our porch, the milk freezes and pushes
up the cardboard cap. Then cream rises
out of the top of the bottle
like ascending to the sky where heaven is
over the porch and lilac tree.

But milk isn't sinful
like my father's brown beer, milk is white
and comes from cows. Cows don't sin.

Cows don't hate anybody either.
They're not mean,
don't hit their cousins like I hit

my cousin Mavis who gave me me a doll
for my birthday instead of a cap gun.
And cows don't say no to their mother
or start to wet the bed again like me, do they?
No, they don't!

Away far and hot is the war
where Father went. Snow doesn't fall
there, so soldiers don't need to shovel
the sidewalk. In war country
Jesus doesn't send snow to cover
people's sins so they cry and cry.
Bombs fall to kill some children
because they're punished for sin
and lie down in fields, never,
never get up because Jesus says
suffer the little children. Some war children
don't have to wake up early and eat oatmeal
before school. You know why?
Because they don't have houses
to sleep in or food to eat, not even crusts,
and there's no school.

Not anymore. In war country the sky
is smoky from burning,
but maybe children can still rise
to be angels because Jesus says come
unto me. Their sky is not blue like ours.
Father's eyes are blue
as heaven.

When the slide melts I put my sleigh away.
Mother climbs the steps to the clothesline,
hangs sheets in the spring air, not in the basement
where they smell like coal from the furnace
all winter.

One afternoon, two special mailmen
knock at the door. They say
they're sorry Father isn't coming home
from the war. Mother holds
a letter with the edge black as sin.
She tells me Father found Jesus
in war country. I say she's happy
Father found Jesus and won't drink beer
or play cards on Sunday anymore,
but she gets mad, and hits me,
then cries and cries.

My aunts come, and my cousin Mavis
and all they do is wail and pray and make tea
because my father's in heaven.
I don't want to cry. I want to find my father.
I go out and lie on green grass to look
up through the lilacs. No birds sing.
I look high over the porch
to see Father in heaven
but the sky is empty.

Prince

Here's an old photo
of my little brother,
Mother's prince

standing on the porch
near a wall
of red hollyhocks.

Look how he turns his face
from the camera
hangs his royal head,

tries not to cry. *Smile,*
I said, *why don't you smile?*

Look how sun shines
on the pink patches
where I shaved his cowlicks

to the scalp to stop his hair
from rising like filigree gold
in a crown.

When Mother saw him
she wept, said
he'd never be the same.

I told her she was wrong.
His hair grew back
almost blond.

But she never forgave me
and we were never
the same.

Sweet

In the old photo
my Greek grandmother sits straight
on her chair
in our Montreal backyard
sucking a lollipop, mouth closed,
white hair pinned back
forties style, ankles crossed.
A widow's black crepe
covers her knees.

Her future lounges nearby
barefoot in lawn chairs
two skinny grandgirls all legs
and scabbed knees.

Heat bakes the brick wall.
Sparrows keep silent
in the spirea hedge.
Three o'clock. Dead hour.
Sunday afternoon.
Three cherry lollipops.

Repentance

Grandpa weeps in the old farmhouse, frets thin fingers
on the blanket covering his head. His face sags,
death-grey. He worries about meeting Grandma
in the beyond, he worries he won't have time to settle
his account with the Baptist God, fierce bringer
of cloud by day, fierce sender of fire
by night

Grandpa's teeth shake in his mouth
like loose stones. He broods on wanderers who traded
Egyptian wheat for manna in the wilderness,
cursed God, repented, and offered the ox.
Smoke rose bright and alive
from the flames, an odour pleasing
to a forgiving Lord.

I don't know about Grandpa's God,
but Grandma knew all along
about his women, kept her years of icy silence,
never forgave him.

Now he wants to burn the girls who hunted seed
inside his barn when he was young, lay open
their wanton thighs, their perfect breasts,
and beg for fire to consume his offering,
lift its saving fragrance
into his dying air.

Baptism

City workers stream from office towers
after work, a filthy human river
unlike the Bow water winding pure
beneath the bridge.

I wait in Starbucks for one who desires
holiness like Agatha, red hair tucked
under her blue cap, Agatha
who turned from the crowd
to watch me recite Bible verses,
stir honey in my tea.

I offered her the holiness she longed for
the gift of new life. How could I have known
she was one more drop in an impure flood
of those who taunt me, laugh and walk by,
leaving me broken.

I led Agatha to redemption, offered her
atonement for sin, but as I knelt with her
under the bridge in the Bow's sacred current
she turned away, fought me crying,
begged me to let her go.

I held her down, gave her the peace
she sought, and in sorrow, lit a candle
for her later in my room. I forgave her
with my blessing. On my altar
I laid her blue cap.

Village

They tell me
a priest
rules the town,

takes the village
pulse
from his rectory window,

has certain sacraments
up his leg,

and a red hot church.

I can imagine
the village women
breaking open like the sky
at noon.

O eagle.
O Saint Francis.

Mattress Salesman

I buy Mum the low profile weave mattress
she needs to serve Jesus in sleep.
Bioflex helps her hear secrets he whispers
through pocketed coils.
On every mattress I sell Mum spreads prayer
like an invisible sheet—on the slip-coil
and foam core, so my customers rest
with the Lord who has nowhere
to lay his head. (Matthew: 8, verse 20.)

Cousin Maude wants me to lay my head
beside hers on a no-noise foam mattress
but if Mum tells the Lord
he might send the boils he sent Dad
for that sin or the plagues that fell
on the house of Pharoah.

The body sheds 40,000 skin cells a minute.
A mattress can fill with micro-bugs.
The foam core self-cleanses, of course,
but mites can invade. The Lord has warned
Mum that even the best mattress breeds mold
and eggs in the coils, stains of sin.

What if the Lord's avengers feed
on my arms and legs in the dark, crawl
into my ears and mouth if I climb
inside Maude? Will the Lord's invisible army
rise then too?

Baby

Door opens wide as crying.
Beloved carries you down,
down you go now bad monkey,
legs and arms crawling
to the only chair in the world
to touch the hair and eyes of Beloved.
You climb, her hand strikes, you fall
like red beads on a string sucked
sour, a fall down wet monkey girl,
dirty diaper girl.

Where does Beloved go
when she opens a new door,
how can you find her
outside here, rain hitting
your head, wind sailing
your breath away?

Morning. Wet crib. Hold the string,
let go, red beads over the rail tumble
down and down to the floor
where you can't climb
to reach one-eyed monkey.
Rain hits the window like a smack.
Stand, shake the bars,
wail, stop, sleep.

You'll lose one-eyed monkey,
forget red beads like blood on your lip.
You won't remember Beloved's hand

striking your face
how many times you fell
before you stood on two feet,
learned to run faster than rain
from room to room searching
for her voice.

You'll mourn the lifetime
you've spent waiting for a Beloved to open
the door wide as crying and lift you
out of your crib.

Reflection

How small we seem, our dark shapes moving
from the house across a winter field
beneath the great sky's shifting circle,
a cloud-caught moon sweeping
interrupted light
over snow.

We keep silent as we walk, wondering
why we possess no light of our own,
need each other's eyes
to see our faces.

Here in this field, we might look back, watch
starlight spill into the empty footsteps
we leave behind.

Here in this field, we might feel our loneliness
and love one another again.

Instead we turn, eager for a lighted house,
like cold children who lose their way
on a dark night, journeying
to the edge of their world.

Word

April. I wait for lilacs to blossom.
Rain fattens buds for May blooms.
Soon wind will scent the air—again—
dangerous purple, dangerous white.

I wait in the branches of this birthing tree.
I will attend the flower flood, watch it open
and rise, crest toward me like the future,
spilling grief, spilling desire.

I will live again when April turns her face
to May, when blossoms on the lilac tree declare
a truce with winter and new leaves, green
on the maple, bring equanimity.

This is the way of grief: living rain journeys
along the dark branch, as prayer journeys
through an unhealed wound, tending loss,
defeating death with a word.

Gardener

The toolshed key opens
memory's door
to a rusted spade, a hoe, old seed,
your kiss blooming like a red tulip
in my palm.

I know rain will fall all day.

I still wear your name
inside my garden glove.

Cosmos seeds lie buried
in the backyard
but not many shoots rise
through the stones
you planted,
not many flowers blossom
where love comes from.

Mourning

The birch tree leans into the wind.
Leaves fall, autumn's pale alms
into the empty palm
of mourning
into the sleeping garden where seed
we scattered last spring
bloomed into a field
of cosmos.

You moved away, didn't stay
for the flowers to open.

Your smile is no longer for me,
but I think of you,
warm in your country,
our separate landscapes
beneath one sky.

Wild Card

I am an unthorned rose
a wingless hummingbird
a wild card played late
a dreaming soul.

I am a wingless hummingbird
a dark room, a ceiling of broken stars
a dreaming soul
a lightning strike.

I am dark room, a ceiling of broken stars
a scarlet maple leaf
a lightning strike
a shadow fading by the door.

I am a scarlet maple leaf
I am a slow clock
a shadow fading by the door
a voice, a wave breaking.

I am a slow clock
a wild card played late
a voice, a wave breaking,
an unthorned rose.

Katsura

In the cemetery I visit
the Katsura tree,
its leaves falling gold
from crown to ground
a halo around the stem.

I breathe the fragrance rising
from these broken leaves
into the wide air
above the graves,
aroma of sugar
defying the bitterness
of death.

Legends say bodies of saints
dying in holiness release
perfume for living faithful
to adore.

I am not a believer, but I kneel
beside this tree, gather
its dead leaves

and bury my face in my hands
to taste their sweet odour
of sanctity.

Tide

I thank the sea for leaving me behind on shore
among this assembly, this synod of shell
and pooled seaweed
abandoned by tide.

The moon is a jealous lover, like God, who pulls
me into His waters leaving me moon-drenched
and sea-flung, borne by a spring tide
that brings my life to its knees.

Whenever I rise and walk again,
sand fills my shoes.
I reek of wrack and algae here,
sea-hymns pool
on the page.

Falling

December embraces maples,
last leaves fall blood-brown
on bleached grass.

A sparrow falls
where your stone opens
the field.

The longest day
of the year falls
before snow.

Song

There is a maple in my yard
where sparrows fly every morning
at dawn.

All summer they sing beneath leaves

but now that the branches are bare
they look like dark buds
blossoming out of season.

Even in January the tree trembles
with their song—
imagine—small birds
shaking light
out of a dead sky.

Gratitude

for Rosemarie

A gull's cry enters
my dream, waves struggling
dawn after dawn.
Stars fade and moon,
the air catches fire
on streets, gardens,
leads bees the way
into lilies
white columbine.
Light through the curtain
rests on our hands
and faces, blessing this day
this beginning.

Raven

I am a hollow log wrapped in moss
an ear listening beneath
a dying tree.

In sleep my dreams hover on nightmare.
Around me last year's leaves
fall.

An owl's cry declares me stranger lying here
among roots and rain, feeding
on wind, wound
in old vines.

From an ancient fir
raven tugs on my life's green thread
unravels moss from my grave, crying

Wake! Wake!

Close

The one you want is not far.
The one you search for
is here, too close to see.
Touch your palm, feel it lead
to knuckle, finger, nail.

Clap your hands
until they ache. For joy.
Raise the morning blind
see a hummingbird taste light
for the first time,
needle beak sun-sugared.

Clap your hands
until they bleed for the raven's fall
to field in mid-flight, broken
like the sparrow
lying among bloodweed
and sage.

Remember the slapped hand,
naughty fingers touching yourself
in the holy unholies.

Remember the hand numbed
by fear and desire beside
a man's ice heart, hand burned
by love's fire for your child,
hand resting on the woman's
soft breast.

No road leads you away
from this room. No knife, no sword
brings you absence.
You have met your hands.
They cover tears on a face dying.
You are already here.

Feedlot

Beneath a cold sky he sits in a truck watching
cramped feedlot cattle stamp snow and earth
under their hooves, their breath
columns of steam in the blue air.

From the window of the truck, he muses on the patience
of animals gazing through squares of frozen
chain-link fence, eyes fixed as meditators
on the eternity of a man sitting in a truck
on a road.

From the window of the truck, he imagines the cattle
know their world will close tomorrow
or the next day, depending on the speed range
of the slaughter line.

Then he figures that animals don't understand
any more than he does how shock and stun
can shut a life down the way a door does
when it's slammed in a face
or a marriage does when it slips
down the back stairs after all these years

or why thoughts come to him now of dead cattle hanging
on hooks while he sits here freezing at the edge
of a road, head resting on the wheel
of a stalled truck.

Winter

for Pam and Larry

In the parking lot behind our building
snow falls

on the couple walking together
from a van.

Their hands are empty, but when they turn
to each other and smile

I imagine branches of wild orange blossoming
in their arms

fragrance of petals blessing
the cold air.

I open my window.

Look!

Lovers are passing by
scattering grace.

Catherine

They in fair heaven nest
~ David Taylor, *Easter Poem*

From fair heaven's nest
like a branch-shaken wren
you fell off the edge
of childhood
onto the stone wings
of the family's
punishing God.

Birds befriended you
ducks, sky-weary geese
who flew back to the cottage
each spring to hear
mother goose tales
you told them
in your garden.

Starved raptor,
a brother craved flight
crawled up neon stairs
to rooftops, skin wallet
heavy with monopoly money
throat ragged with rage
and strike.

He imagined
he'd left you behind
beloved sister,

and you believed him
though you were the one
who carried the dove
the one who found light
on the face
of our dying mother.

Requiem

My Dear Count

Last night I slept at my desk having written
only to the eighth bar of the *Kyrie*, despite
your kind advance, which went to debt.
By day, I serve at a jam factory to buy bread
and coal for my wife and children.
Salzburg winter blows against our door
but if Your Grace might provide
a second advance, I shall deliver
The Requiem by April.

W A Mozart

Bootsteps strike cold cobbles behind me—
the ghost of my father—
I cough.

Miserere

At the factory, bright carts from Italy
ripe plums in my apron,
red grapes, sun on my work-bench—
apricots warm and peaches
notes on the wood-staves rolling to chords—
melody runs—juice through my fingers.

Sanctus

The foreman laughs, *You sing
like an altar boy.*

Fruit falls to the vat
floats sweet to the boil,
against the iron like a bell
the jam pole tolls.

Benedictus

The Poet

for Daniel Scott

In the dark times
Will there also be singing?
Yes, there will be singing
About the dark times.
~ Bertolt Brecht, *Motto*
Svendborg Poems

A last syllable lies
on the poet's page, but a voice
reaches his ear later at the mirror,
later in a dream, a door leads
down stone steps
in seething dark
a mute soul weeps
for lost words:

> Thunder flies inside me, sails
> my voice to Saturn's moons.
> I spin in the gas of nine rings
> without hope of return, the Titan grasps
> my arms, his breath burning my hand
> here in the planet's basement I can't speak,
> cold ashes bind my mouth.

The poet waits in darkness.
When the words find him
he is no longer harmless
his poems are dangerous.

Artist

after Giselle

On the beach, an artist carves objects
from driftwood: turtles and frogs, a stairway
to heaven, a heart, all gifts
from the sea.

For the dwellings he builds, he polishes stones
left on sand for his hands
to gather.

Late afternoon. I look at the ocean
whose waves struggled to shore
before we were born
and whose tides will ebb
and rise again here
after we're gone.

Eve

*Nothing is what it seems
through this glass eye.*
~ P. K. Page, *Kaleidoscope, II.
A Little Reality*

Nothing is what it seems through this glass eye
refracting a world outside Eden,
you and the man
eating despair.

Nakedness, shame, nothing looks true
through this eye, rough hands
pulling sons from your body,
old age, promise of pain,
death.

Your eye already scorns the man whose rib
you wear, the one swaying drunk
at the gate, blaming you for his exile
to a thistled field where violence
breeds murder.

Beyond the exit, see how the serpent bellies
away undercover. See the man vomiting
in a field of thorns.
Light of the garden fades.

All your life you'll mourn this loss,
beg God, wrestle angels at the portal
and burn your hands on fire-swords
guarding the gate.

All your life you'll plead for light
and wisdom to flood your blindness
with the radiance you lost
in paradise.

Blessing

After such knowledge, what
forgiveness?
~ T.S. Eliot, *Gerontion*

Bend an ear to the grass, kneel under a fir
like a child, weave columbine in your hair
and ask for the blessing
of earth.

You'll be eager to hear you're wolf and raven,
ocean and sky, a moonstone stolen from rain
an altar of grass, the oak
under whose branches
you dream.

But when you hear you're the bite
of your own sharp tooth on your hand,
the sting of your own
slapped face

you will wake and wonder where you can hide
from such knowledge, what forgiveness
there is for you

now that you are the blessing you begged
to receive, the woman
you've waited a lifetime
to love.

Lovers

Lovers on winged feet,
we sped across the stone floor,
petals spilling from our arms.

Light filled our bed as we led
each other blindfolded, singing
into love's jurisdiction.
Fragrance of lilac blessed the air,
in our garden beneath the window
sun seduced the apple tree,
our cries blossomed
all summer.

We believed in those days
that love belonged to us, we had no idea
of love's law, could not imagine
that the child's death in winter
would tie our frozen hands together,
fasten us like prisoners
to judgment's bare tree,
and that when we looked, we'd see
a ruined branch
and turn our grieving faces
away from each other.

In those years, we had no idea
of love's law, could not imagine
that in time, mercy would unbind
our wrists, release us
into each other's custody,

and that there could come
the gift sometimes given
to lovers who endure loss: the grace
to turn and see the wounded branch,
see the green leaf open.

Sea Change

White waves break over your hair
sea weed curls in your hand
salt crystals shine in the air.

A north wind storms our affair
and you lie warm on the strand
white waves break over your hair.

You tell me life is not fair
rough seas beat against us on land
salt crystals shine in the air.

You're sorry you no longer care,
you tell me time runs like the sand
white waves break over your hair.

Your wind-borne words tear
at the sea wall where I stand
salt crystals shine in the air.

You swim away and I must bear
my grief for everywhere on land
white waves break over your hair
salt crystals shine in the air.

Affair

I fasten a rope
between our houses
and I wait

All day
the wren sits
on the sundial
and whistles
for evening

Night comes
and I watch
for her

Wind lifts
her blouse
her hair

It is not until
she steps
carefully
from the roof
that I think
of Icarus falling
toward
a dark sun.

The Visit

On the day I moved out
I placed flowers on the hall table
so that the room would seem less cold
when you returned
and heard my footsteps
echoing on the icy stairs,
the door closing early
like a winter sky.

Now, on the anniversary
of my leaving,
I watch you climb the snow-bank alone,
daffodils spilling from your arms
as you run toward me.

You have heard that graves can open
in spring, like petals.

Passage

I push snow on the long walk
with an old shovel my ex forgot
to take with him when he left me
for a taller woman.

I hurry so medics can race to the house
in case my son stops breathing
like he did one night
last winter.

Snow sticks to the blade of the shovel's
jagged rim. If I were taller,
I could tilt it over the towering bank
but I can't reach
that high.

I want to rest, but if I stop now
I'll see myself:

a short woman fastened to a ruined shovel
losing her way to the road.

Goodbye

You wandered away from the crushed car,
the cutting jaws of life, touch and go
it was for her then, and the child,

ambulance lights flare-red, blinked on dark tar
like animal eyes. The motor slowed,
a faltering heart.

Black ice, the curve it was, not you shivering
on the median, trying to catch your breath
for the test, the air so cold
your hands couldn't remember
how to say *later,* or
see you.

She left you anyway, didn't she?
called *see you later,* running down
the steep stairs, *see you soon,*
stumbling out of the marriage again
through the back lane to the shelter
like last time, the child hung
over her shoulder, wailing
into the jaws of sky

goodbye

goodbye

Admonitions

A woman must not use fire to cleanse knives
lest bread burn the tongue of her husband.
She must not wear a red gown to a pigsty
lest bacon bleed in the fire.

A woman must not climb a tower
lest her pride rise and shame her husband.
She must not uncover her hair in August
lest hail falls, destroying the wheat.

Should a dog enter her dwelling after rain,
a woman must not kiss his ears or genitals
to conceive, for she will bear a deaf infant
with a long tail.

During a drought, a woman with child
may collect lamb's urine for her thirst
but she may not drink the urine of a ram
lest her newborn sprout horns.

A woman must not weave curses into the pocket
of her husband's cloak, nor poison his ale
nor serve him the crust of blue bread
lest he rave and burn down the village.

A woman must not rub afterbirth on the cock
of her son, lest he take fright and his manhood fail.
But a woman may spread afterbirth on the breasts
of her daughter that she may conceive.

A woman who learns to read will ride away
from her husband's dwelling. If a woman learns
to write, says Llamnrun, blessed be his name,
an elder shall cut off her hand.

Early Love Notes

A loathsome ague plots to keep thee hence
With burning bones and head; it maketh sense
To cease awhile amid this baneful woe
And all reunions quit, research foregoe
'Til thou art well; and please thee, physick keep
For as the heart needs love, the flu needs sleep.

How now, my love? Dost thou again fare well
Since last upon thine e-mail I did glance?
O that these lines could all thy fevers quell
And cool thy cheek and give dear spirit chance
To laugh aloud upon such human lot
As catches flu just when her heart would not!

I turn my waking eyes upon thy face
To gaze on thee, who sleep'st in morning's grace,
And bid thee wake with quiet words and light
Restored to me refreshed by dreams of night.
So as a gift shall I thee this day give
That thou in healthful joy, and love may live.

How can'st thou welcome night, the dying day
When nature's watch must summer's light release
And on bright hills and fields, a carpet lay
For darkness and his shadowed steps' increase?
How can'st thou praise that time when we must part
Yet claim thou lov'st me with an honest heart?

Slowly I turn my thoughts away from thee
To gaze on sleep, for sleep doth beckon me
With quiet song, with notes so soft and clear
That I need follow her, though thou be near.
But in my dreams I shall thine image find
And love thee still whom I must leave behind.

Break-up in F#

Phyllis! flock off
you frock,

get the flack
out of my face, Phyllis
you fork.

I don't give a flying fix.
Go freak yourself!
I don't give a frying flog!

Don't flake where you freaking
flax, Phyllis
just fake off,

and take your flack
the flog out of my friction,
for frock's sake.

Who the fax are you
anyway, Phyllis? you flocking
flake.

You're off freight!
Now get the frolic out.
You're forking fiction,

Phyllis!

Apology

Don't slay me Phyllis. Put the knife away
and grate the peel you need for key lime pie,
or serve that maple mousse. It's not the day
to stab me in the heart and watch me die.
Please slice your lemon tart while I explain.
The angry speaker wrote the line, it's she
who told you to flock off; so don't complain.
I'm not to blame for what she said. You see,
the words were hers; you know my love is true,
much sweeter than your apple squares, your cake.
Don't hurt me, Phyl. I'd never say, 'frock you.'
Let's eat cream tarts, the macaroons you bake.
Please use your blade to slice the nutmeg flan,
and let me live to polish off the pan.

Bounty

A lady wearing white teeth and a white apron
over her gown carries a roll
of paper towel.

Actors gather for the commercial.

Here's the scene: the lady has twenty seconds
to tear a sheet, blot chocolate cake batter
the daughter sprays on the kitchen counter.
Thirty seconds to wipe away the blackberry yoghurt
the schoolboy knocks over with his backpack.

One sheet swipes both.

The husband enters.
His glass of orange juice breaks in his hand,
splashes near the fridge,
and blood spatters on cupboard doors,
the baby's face.

Forty seconds, two sheets.

The lady's smile flashes
she tears the towel for the next mishap.

And I want her to mop up my life.

Unfurl your roll, O Lady of Bounty,
for my coffee stains and grape jam smears,
my tidal divorces, dripping egg yolks,
the tears that stream down my face

and pool on the kitchen table
when police bring the news
about my son.

Empty

I want to be an empty room
now that we've burned
each other's flags,
worn out our battle.

When you kicked down
the door and fled,
in rushed neighbours
to carry away my silver bowl
of oranges, the crystal flutes,
the bottle of Dom Perignon
I was saving for you.

Now they press glasses
to the wall to hear me war
with myself, listen to me
rage and weep.

I want to be an empty room
with a locked door, my window
open only to the holly tree,
the bird-ringed sky.

Fisher

I stood on the landing
and looked for your boat
near the stream falling
out of the mountain.
I saw her troll with you,
pull on your oar.

He's caught a new girlfriend,
a fly fisher told me
tying his lure.

I shook off my sandals,
shed my red dress,
gills grew from my ribs, then fins,
a ridge wound green
down my spine
like a tail.

At sunset scales gleamed
on my breasts
and when the sky closed,
I slipped in dark water
and flowed to the shore
where you landed me,
fastened your gold hook
in my mouth.

Voicemail

A wolf is tearing a carton of ice cream
in my living room right now, waiting for me
to pour the melted chocolate.

Sorry, I can't take your call.

I could ask her to pause while I clean the spill
from the carpet, but she cracked my hand
in her jaw earlier and wants to feed me
chocolate mousse to soothe the pain.

I can't talk until the ice cream's gone, even then
she'll rip the stuffed turkey carcass
in the fridge, the package of Oreos
in the cupboard.

There's no telling when I'll be free to help you.
Perhaps tomorrow.

But I can't promise.
I know this wolf.

She's starving.

Gift

The ceiling broods like a false sky
above your head. In the mirror

your face fades, hands curl
on the arms of your chair.

You are time's prisoner
you say, your light fails

like the fire whose ashes lie cold
in the grate, grey as the door

you have locked, grey
as the walls of the room

where you live with yourself
inside the barred window.

If you were a believer
you would ask ancient gods

for a gift, perhaps the peacock
beloved of Hera,

invite him to enter the bars
of your room trailing starlight

and hyacinths into your darkness.
If you were a believer

he would arrive moments
from now, stand iridescent

beside the chair where you sit
trying to forget who you are,

he would gaze at you, immortal,
hundred eyes luminous,

sacred feathers burning
blue fire.

Ophelia I

A stallion stamps under a tree
in the back yard meadow.

At the casement she dreams
he gallops to fill
the nothing
she holds in her arms
with blood flowers, weeds
for her hair.

Walls of the palace whisper
her name, tell the tale
of a stallion wakening
dangerous
under a yew tree,
fennel and columbine
tangling his mane.

She wants him to ride her
past dreams and stones
in the wall, past curtains
waving goodbye

past the field, away to his bed
of wild grass near a stream
that's not there.

Ophelia II

Poor Ophelia! What could you do,
armed only with youth
and frail beauty,
without wisdom of hilt or shaft,
sans dagger,
sans rapier for your moon-pale hand
in a cold Danish palace
where swords rang
steel against stone walls,
where a royal ghost
crying for revenge
drowned your sweet song.

Helpless to avenge your father's death,
or challenge four acts of mind games
played by the dallying prince
you loved, you found madness.

No wonder you wound fennel
and columbine into your hair, and veiled
like a bride, sped on the path
to wed water, lay yourself down
on the altar of virgins
disappointed in love.

Had you fled to a nunnery, wed God,
you might have lived to brood
on the play, pray for the souls
of all those who lay dead
at the end of Act V.

Blinds

We design booklet shapes for single doors, with shades
ranging from triple opaque to single translucency.

For double doors our home shapes pull power-rise
battery shades.

When triple doors take triple shapes, we offer
patio battery shades, cordless-operated.

For single rooms we design single translucent windows
with options for triple-door shapes.

We single the doors for efficiency with double options,
and triple cords for rooms with windows.

Children? for children see: design.maybe@thankfully.com
For children we offer honeycomb.

Journey

A woman on the bus tells me
she's going to visit her daughter. In hospital.
Holds up a pink T-shirt, says
there's still time.

I want the driver to turn the wheel,
cross the median,
carry her back to the years she's come from.

I want her to call her child's name
again and again so we'll remember
the name like a song we heard
one morning on the way to work.

The bus rides down Côte des Neiges hill.
I watch the St. Lawrence winding below us
under a cold sky.
I want to tell the woman
about my teenage son
who took a shortcut through a train yard
last winter

but think it's better to point out
that the ice on the river is breaking,
that we can see water
moving again—in places—
its blue flow.

Doe

Vulture wings a black circle
over the house,
his eyes pierce siding
what lies beneath stud,
bone, aging flesh,
the body's failing liver.

I am an uninvited guest
in my own life.
A stranger.

When my lover left, she took
my words with her.
I don't remember
my name.

Wallpaper, floor, rust and mold,
at the door, footprints,
blood trail.

Were the stains here
when my lover moved out?

Did someone carry a dying doe
into these rooms on his shoulder,
conceal a shot animal here?

On the roof, vulture peers
into the gaping skylight, talons
pace the hours.

I will find the doe before dark,
bathe her wound and golden eyes
I will sing a name
to her broken heart.

From her skin's tawny sheen
the odour of death will not rise.

Not here.

Raid

Montréal, 1957

I didn't care when my ex warned me
about the old butch
leaning against the rail in the Peel Street gay bar
blowing smoke rings into the red light whirl,
the one looking for a new girl
to sit on her lap all night.

I knew she'd bury her hands in my shirt, hurt me
the way I wanted, so I sat on her knees listening
to Tangerine sing *Cry me a River* in the key of real tears,
mascara streaming out of her eyes like black light.

My new dyke and me were too busy to run
when cops swooped in after midnight,
grabbed queers, loaded us in a paddy wagon
so we'd lose our jobs on Monday, our names
on the front page of *The Gazette*.

Eh! Chiens!

So there's me and my new dyke on the bench
in the wagon, her hands singing into me, cops panting
like backup, one of them yelling at the driver
to take the long way down rue Ste. Catherine.

What with me crying, and my new dyke moaning
out of tune, we give cops a night-shift thrill
all the way to the station.

I remember thinking, what a crazy story.
Maybe I'll write it down when I'm old
if I feel like living that long.

Conductors

A St. Lawrence Valley farmer
mounts rods on his barn

to catch the lightning
when it strikes

to lead the lightning
underground.

He says I should taste
the beans, the electrified
squash.

I have begun to wear a
tongue stud

in case a poem
strikes.

Communion

Raven patrols the road,
a gull on the roof of the Hotel Rialto watches sky.
Both birds spy a wind-blown wrapper
on Douglas Street. Gull dives,
white wing, black wing. War.

Raven eats the crust.
Bad bird!
calls a good boy—*thief!*—

Mother covers his eyes. Gull wheels
misfortune back to his roof
crying doom.

When I was small, a church raven perched
on a stained glass window ledge
and cawed my name. One Sunday,
he stole a sermon on sin from the Reverend's mouth,
thieved the choir's mournful hymn.

I prayed for beak-sharp teeth, blue-black wings
to grow on my shoulders.
Hungry, unholy, I learned to beat
sweet brother
to the kitchen floor and feed on the scraps
our mother dropped
of love.

Beach

Look how the waves carry these logs to shore!
They fall like sea-worn arms and legs of Titans torn
in battle under an ancient sky.

I can almost hear swords ring on the wind
that rips the fiery sails of their sinking ship,
see the current run with warrior blood.

Now, their story lost, forgotten, the broken limbs lie
wrapped in bull-whip kelp on the beach
where sunburned boys build them into forts.

From wreckage brought by tides, these children
fashion spears of splintered wood, arming
themselves for war.

They watch the strait all afternoon, waiting
for an enemy to rise out of the water, and run
toward them.

They want to be ready, still eager for the kill
when night falls.

Storm

In a night window on Menzies
cook shakes a wok over flame,
aroma of new rice pours
into wind and rain.

When I was a child you fed me,
my mouth at your breast.

A bus carries me to my room, a bed
a cup of tea, a chair near the window
locked against wind,
against rain.

My life storms. I am an old child
without craft, without oar
my days drown
one after the other.

Dark sea, companion of sleep, shatters
the window, floods my floor
carries me out on its tide.

Reach for me, Mother,
with starlit hands pull me
from your body's dark waves
bring me to life again
in your arms.

Feed me your fire.

Wave

Tsunami, 2011

This is for the child
Who didn't make it
Whose parents tried to drive him
To higher ground
But got the timing wrong
It wasn't their fault they couldn't cipher
The speed of water
Running faster
Than despair
Or the heart's race,
The sleek sea-wave
Already breathing
Their air, riding and riding
Like the fastest horse
The child could imagine galloping after him
The sky pouring stars into his eyes
Mother lifting him
Higher and higher
In her arms
Father's face suddenly dark
The highway drowning
In the rear-view mirror
And ahead, the hills,
the sun going down.

Border

The man's loose boot soles flap
like his heart as he pulls his cart along
a sunburned road.

He doesn't know which side of the war he runs from
who's captured his village, ruined his field
or which soldiers are planting spikes
like a dead fence across the border ahead,
whether the last border he crossed
is closed now, or lost to another army.

On the cart behind him his wrapped wife rides
holding their child's head in her hands
in case gunfire opens the sky over the road.

Running is not hard for the man. What's hard
is how fear sways the cart
in the wrong direction, turns
the road without him.

He can no longer remember who to hate,
whose name
to call out for help
now that the border spins in circles
farther and farther
from any way out of here.

Boot Lesson

You're old enough to wear my boots
for your journey.

Sit.

Thread the aglets through the lower eyelets
until the laces are even
on both sides.

Now cross the aglets back and forth
all the way to the top.

Pull them tight.
Tie the double knot.

Money and the photograph are hidden
between the inner and outer sole
of the left boot.

Remember this,
because Mother and I
won't be there to remind you.

We can't travel that far.

But you—you'll be able to walk all the way
through the woods
in these boots—

all the way to the border
without falling.

Saga

In Oslo young gods jog
early in winter to the harbour
past ships named Wotan, Thor,
old scorchers
of the fjord's ice trail

I'm not a young god,
I wait for the bells
of Saint Olaf's to ring noon
before I reach
for my cane, shake my eiderdown
into the pearl light.

Most afternoons I ride to a bistro
to read *The Sagas* and drink hot wine
with office girls wild as Freyja
tall as blue-eyed Astrild
who come on break to smoke
and flirt.

They see I burn for them
recalling their divine heat,
but they know well
that when night winks
in the darkness
only young gods will lie in the fire
between their blond legs
while this old god
snores.

Madame Gagnon

May, 1941

Sun filled the garden
when Borduas arrived
to paint your portrait.

Shall I sit by the window,
Jean-Paul?

Non, Madame Gagnon.

Black mix for your dress,
a forest green thread
to your *décollété*, scarlet lip,
rose ochre
arm and cheek.

He brushed midnight into your hair
at noon, ebony in your eyes,
and over your dark head
and shoulders, a bright
angle, the moonlit arc.

When you saw his art
you wondered
who you were.

Years later I visit your portrait
in the Borduas Gallery.
If I gaze at you long enough,
I might learn how to look
at my lover, see her
as Borduas saw you, Madame Gagnon
when he moved your chair
from a bright window to find
your darkness
and paint your light.

Still

I squat in the desert and wait
To deliver you.

Wind wraps the sun around me
Like a burning sheet.

Soon I will break the vulture's grasp
With my steel hand,

Watch a night jackal run
From my flame.

Stones sharpen my teeth.
I will sever the cord.

I will carry you home

In my skirt, the thin white blouse
I have torn with my nails.

Let no one come near me.
Let no one hear

The sound I make when I deliver you
And you are not born.

History

Kids at school laughed, said he stank like squirrel stew
or mouse shit, like an old suitcase, man,
smell of the country he came from
maybe it was the sweater his grandmother knitted
in her old kitchen, garlic and wild leek, the rabbit
she caught, boiling in a pot on the peat hearth,
needles clicking smell into the wool
row after row.

He threw the sweater in a dumpster on the way home from school.
Bought a new one, red, white and blue
at the five and dime with paper-route money
but the kids still laughed. He thought
something inside his skin must reek through the pores
of his big hands, thin chest,
maybe his grandmother's life poured
out of his mouth with every breath his heart pumped,
a foreign smell, stink in his blood, her stories living
in him, old words knitted beneath new.

New words came to him in pieces
but when he strung them together, he smelled shame
for the place he'd come from, his grandmother's childhood
on the farm, her hands old at ten, look.
How the soil starved during the war, *malchik,* she said.
Acorns and thistles.

And how, when she fled, the child she carried on her back
lived almost to the border.
Your uncle, she cried. *Before your father was born,*
listen, malchik, weeping in her new kitchen
trying to reach him
trying to knit their worlds together.

Exodus

I sit in the garden wondering
why my owners chased me
out of the villa, left me alone
in the dark,
why they fled after someone
killed Sethos, the eldest.
Perhaps no one's left
inside the barred chambers.

Across the garden wall,
no river runs
through the bleached field
where enemy slaves of Pharaoh,
pull their tents
from the stone-strewn soil.

I climb the wall.
I have nowhere else to go
and these slaves
might be traveling east
to a better country.

If they let me join them,
I'll help gather
food in the mornings, walk
behind their cloud,

and at night, when I'm afraid,
I might learn to trust
that into the cold desert dark
their God will send fire.

Amir's Children

A scientist studying evolution traveled forty miles of rutted road
to a Turkish village looking for the cottage Amir built
to hide his adult children from people who called them dogs
because they walked on hands and feet.

The scientist observed Amir's children near the cottage
at a coop in the mud yard, collecting eggs. They looked like adults
pretending to be children, pretending to be dogs. They wore old shoes
on their hands and feet, slipped down the mud path, watching
for stones.

They looked behind them as they swayed, feet following hands,
but never looked up at the geneticist or the sky over the cottage,
or at the sacks swinging under their hips where eggs rolled, shell
against fragile shell.

The scientist drove Amir's children to a beach, watched them run,
hands bare, feet bare on sand, past seaweed to the water,
crying with joy to touch the sea for the first time, faces lifted
to the waves. When bathers laughed to see them leap
like dogs, the children didn't look up.

The scientist dreamed he wore new shoes on his hands,
new shoes on his feet to journey across a muddy, sea-pooled stage
in Stockholm. When people laughed, applauded to see a dog
accept the Nobel prize, he dreamt he wept, and didn't look up.

Home

I ask Mother how far wind travels
to kiss the hem of wet sheets
hung like sails on the line.
I want to know such things.

At dusk I gather sweetgrass sailboats
from the cloud-scattered field
so river can hurry them
home to the sea.

Mother carries dry linens
away from the line,
calls me home before evening
brings darkness
inside the cottage.

Fragrance of sweetgrass covers my bed,
honeysuckle blown from the meadow.

I want to know how wind tells
my name to the moon
how the moon sails home.

Corrida

Memory circles the arena, cuts
into an unhealed wound, a mother's
black shawl, a story, bull raging
the first lance.

Memory, red as blood and fear,
mother running down sun-baked hill
searching for her boy, finds him
gathering waves in his small hands,
sea blessing the shore
where he kneels.

Memory, the priest gathering
her virginity into his black robe
blood crying, in the vault, eye of God
blinking. Body of Christ.

Memory, circle of years, his boy
acolyte swinging the thurible,
incense rising, rising.

Memory, lilt of his song, glass raised
high for army compadres cheering the bull.
She had no idea he'd grow old enough
for war so soon. Matador drops
a bull's ear, blood petal, the lover's
white palm.

Memory, soldier weeps at her door,
bravest he knew, lying in another country
breathing blood, mouth filled with ash,
altar of home shifting in his eyes
at the end of the nave, a bell
tolling *la muerte*.

Shroud. Evening story, purple cloud
down burned hills to the village square
where Our Lady of Santa Pola sways
on the shoulders of fishermen,
the band's weary tango, memory
flickering in the dark, a boy's candle.

Acknowledgements

These poems or their earlier versions first appeared or will appear in the following publications: *The Fiddlehead, Time of Singing, Our Daily Poem, Mile O Magazine, Island Writer Magazine, Event, The Antigonish Review, Ocean Wilderness Chapbook: berries, (small) and rain, 2012,* and *Planet Earth Poetry Anthology, 2012.*

The poem "History" won a prize in the Victoria Writers' Society Writing Contest, 2012.

Special thanks to past and present mentors who continue to inspire my work: Victoria Adams, Sharon Bezeau, Patrick Lane, Sheila Martindale, David McGimpsey, Wendy Morton, and Chris Schoofs.

Many thanks to Susan Merskey of Goldfinch Press and to Yvonne Blomer of Planet Earth Poetry reading series.

I have been fortunate in my readers and listeners: Deanna Barwick Wall, Sidney Bending, Yvonne Blomer, Catherine Castle, Phyllis Clare, Cris Codman, Miriam Cohen, Kathryn Collins, Sara Courant, Diane Desroches, Zoe Dickinson, Dorothy Goldwater, Carol Halligan, Terry Jones, Elizabeth Johnston, Carol Katz, Helen Knight, Maurice Krystal, Carol Lane, Frank Lemco, Carol McCloskey, Judy McIlmoyl, Ruth Mitchell, Ulrike Narwani, Tris Pargeter, Hilary Phenix, Pamela Porter, Roland Rho, Oritte Rudski, Daniel Scott, and Marlyn Silverstone.

Many thanks to the supportive, encouraging poets of Planet Earth Poetry; to members of the New Horizons Writing Group, and to my fellow poets of the Ocean Wilderness Retreat, March 2012.

Judith Castle lived in Montréal, Québec for many years where she taught Humanities at Collège Lasalle, and Social Psychology at Conted, Concordia University.

Her art photographs have been exhibited at Galerie Luz and Galerie Nota Bene, Montréal.

In November, 2010 she moved to Victoria where she is a volunteer at James Bay New Horizons, and a regular reader at Planet Earth Poetry.

www.judithcastle.com

Printed in Great Britain
by Amazon